FIVE STEPS
TO
FACING SUFFERING

About the
5 Steps Series

The books in the 5 Steps Series are useful for anyone seeking bridge-building solutions to current issues. The 5 Steps series presents positive approaches for engaging with the problems that open up gaps and divisions in family, school, church, and society. Each volume presents five short chapters (or "steps") on a single topic. Each chapter includes a relevant "excerpt" from a prominent writer, "insights" from the author, and an "example" to consider. The "example" is a real-life story that illustrates how each step can be applied in daily life.

FIVE STEPS
TO
FACING SUFFERING

Insights and Examples

Geraldine Guadagno

New City Press
of the Focolare
Hyde Park, New York

Published in the United States by New City Press
202 Comforter Blvd., Hyde Park, NY 12538
www.newcitypress.com
©2014 Geraldine Guadagno

Cover design by Leandro de Leon

Real-life Stories printed with permission from various issues of *Living City* Magazine.

A catalog record is available from the Library of Congress.

ISBN: 978-1-56548-502-0

Printed in the United States of America

*In loving memory
of my mother,
Pauline.*

*Her suffering
was not in vain.*

Contents

Introduction 9

Step 1
Facing the "Why" 13
   Excerpt: Dennis J. Billy, C.Ss.R—
      "Giving Suffering New Meaning" 14
   Example: *A Barrier-Free World* 18

Step 2
Recognizing the Presence of
   Jesus in Suffering 23
   Excerpt: Dietrich Bonhoeffer and Edith
      Stein— "Cooperating with Christ" .. 24
   Example: *Jobless in Texas* 27
   Example: *Illness, Fear and Love* 29

Step 3

Living the Present Moment 31

Excerpt: Thomas Merton and Mahatma Gandhi— "Accepting Suffering in the Present" 32

Example: *I Want What You Want* 35

Step 4

Embracing Jesus Crucified and Forsaken 39

Excerpt: John Paul II — "The Depth of the Mystery" 40

Example: *Competing Deadlines* 44

Example: *Unconditional Love for My Daughter* 45

Step 5

Going beyond Suffering toward Unity with Our Neighbor 49

Excerpt: Chiara Lubich — "The Way to Love Our Neighbor" 50

Example: *An Enduring Love* 55

Notes 59

Further Reading 61

Introduction

On the first anniversary of my father's death, a doctor told me—as gently as he could—that my mother had six months to live. I staggered out of the hospital room like I had been hit with a hammer. Although I was in my early forties and married, it struck me that I was also an only child and about to be orphaned. Hours later, when the shock wore off, I broke down. I never showed my fear or sorrow to my mom, who was prone to anxiety attacks. I wanted to keep her spirits up for as long as I could. So while I helped care for her, I also spent time sharing activities that she could still enjoy, even if it was just watching a "classic" TV comedy. I arranged visits from relatives, friends and a clergyman known for his sense of humor almost as much as his charity. Inwardly and privately, however, I offered my worries and heartache to God. I knew that compared to the trials of many others, mine were very small. And yet, I suffered.

Five Steps to Facing Suffering

It can strike anyone, anywhere, at any time. It can assume many guises: the death of a loved one or the loss of a job, illness or accident, separation or divorce, a natural disaster affecting millions or a lone gunman affecting dozens. We think that we are strong, and we might be. But even something tiny—like a paper cut—can make us suffer. Suffering, like joy, is part of the human condition. We see and hear reports of tragedies from all over the world every day. Whether those events affect us directly or not, we cannot help being moved. Unlike joy, people try to avoid suffering as much as possible. Think of how medical science has developed a cornucopia of drugs to ease all kinds of ailments. We even have prescriptions that can ease empathy-induced sadness and anxiety.

How do we make sense of suffering? How can we best respond to it? Should we fight it? Ignore it? Wish it away? Maybe we could try to give it meaning and even turn it into something positive. This book aims to do just that—give meaning to suffering and transform it into something beneficial, perform a sort of spiritual alchemy.

Suffering has been and will always be a mystery. Mysteries cannot be solved by logic; they lie beyond the intellectual and the physical. Simplistic answers will not do, and I will not offer any. But the steps outlined here do attempt to provide a response to suffering that

Introduction

has proven meaningful in the lives of countless people from varied backgrounds, religious or not.

Although my response stems from Christianity, it also resonates and connects with others developed over centuries within other major religions, and by philosophers or secular thinkers. "All of the world's great religions have found it necessary to address the problem of evil in their most fundamental writings," states the *Dictionary of Bible and Religion*. And further, "In principle, the concept of evil and its close relation, creaturely suffering, would not be problematical were there no concept of good."[1]

In a way, religions, philosophies, even humanism have a common point of intersection: "good," specifically doing good toward others, often by virtue of compassion — which means etymologically "to suffer *with*" — and amid our own sufferings. Buddhism teaches empathy and unconditional love for suffering persons; the one who has transcended suffering needs to help others do the same. Many Hindus believe that suffering is punishment for misdeeds committed in this lifetime or past lives, and so can be remediated by performing good deeds. Many Muslims believe that a suffering neighbor is a test of one's own charity (love) and faith. Judaism also calls for compassionate responses and deeds toward the suffering in an effort to create a better world. Christians, too, are called to love; Jesus gave a new commandment, which he called his own: "Just as I have loved you, you also should love one another" (John 13:34). Whom are they called to love? Matthew's Gospel provides a list of sorts: the hungry, thirsty, or naked, the stranger and the prisoner; in other words, those who suffer (see 25:34-40).

Judeo-Christian tradition and scriptures make it clear that God, who is all-good, did not create suffering or death for Adam and Eve, nor for humanity. In Romans, Chapter 5, Paul says that death entered the world through the sin of one man (Adam). But, God loved us so much that he sent his son, Jesus Christ, to save us from sin. Of course, suffering still exists. How then, today, can we deal with suffering—our own, someone else's and that of the world—with integrity, faithfulness, courage, hope, and maturity? That is what the following pages will explore.

The steps along this journey are (1) facing the "Why"; (2) recognizing the presence of Jesus in suffering; (3) living the present moment; (4) embracing Jesus crucified and forsaken; and (5) going beyond suffering toward unity with our neighbor. A real-life story or two will follow the discussion of each step. In these stories, people like ourselves share how they have grappled with suffering and still do, but have found meaning and transformation walking the Five Steps to Facing Suffering.

Step 1
Facing the "Why"

Giving Suffering New Meaning

Suffering touches everyone. It is part of the human condition, one of the realities of life.…. Dealing with suffering is the heart of the matter. On the most basic level, one that touches every aspect of our lives, each person must decide if suffering has meaning.…. Sometimes the suffering in the world is so overwhelming that it leaves us speechless.

Christian faith affirms that God has not remained silent before the ravages of human suffering. In the person of Jesus Christ, the Word of God himself became flesh, becoming like us in all things but sin (Heb 4:15). In his embrace of the cross he experienced the depth of suffering, giving it new meaning through the power of his selfless love.

Dennis J. Billy, C.Ss.R [2]

Facing the "Why"

WHEN WE SUFFER, WHEN someone we love suffers, or when an entire people suffer, our biggest question is often "Why." Why me? Why my spouse, my child, my parent? Why this disease, that crisis? Why does God our father, who is Love, let his children suffer? People have pondered that question for thousands of years—from the author of the book of Job to twentieth century authors like C.S. Lewis, who offers the following thoughts in *The Problem of Pain:*

> It is men, not God, who have produced racks, whips, prisons, slavery, guns, bayonets and bombs; it is by human avarice ... that we have poverty and overwork. But there remains, nonetheless, much suffering which cannot thus be traced to ourselves. Even if all suffering were man-made, we should like to know the reason.[3]

The unanswerable "Why" can be frustrating, mystifying, infuriating, and even paralyzing. Is there anyone whose experience can help us go beyond this question? Jesus Christ can give us new perspective. Fully divine and fully human, he has penetrated the mystery of suffering.

While he was on the cross, Jesus also asked "Why," just like us. He said, "My God, my God, why have you forsaken me?" (Mk 15:34). Mysteriously, just like us, Jesus received no answer. This is astounding when we consider that God had spoken at Jesus' baptism and at his transfiguration, calling him "my Son, the Beloved" (Mk 1:11 and Mt 17:5). But when on the cross Jesus cried out, the one he called "Abba" — "Dad" — remained silent. In that silence, however, Jesus entrusted himself to God. Despite his own "Why," he also said, "Father, into your hands I commend my spirit" (Lk 23:46).

Those who face the perennial "Why?" can find strength and courage by identifying with Jesus' forsakenness on the cross.

One such person is Chiara Luce Badano, born in Sassello, Italy in 1971. Intelligent, athletic and exuberant, at age sixteen Chiara Badano was struck with cancer. But, several years prior to contracting cancer, she had embraced the gospel and started to put its message into practice. This also included identifying with Jesus' "Why" on the cross. She had learned to identify her own questions with his. This time was no different. Like any normal teenager, after her diagnosis, Chiara shut herself in her room and struggled against being sick. But, just thirty minutes later, she went to her mother and said, "I told him, 'If you want it, Jesus, then I want it, too.' "

Instead of becoming depressed, withdrawn or dependent on painkillers, Chiara offered all her sufferings — from chemotherapy, to losing her hair, to surgery — as a loving response to Jesus. In an effort to reach out to others, she tried to help another young patient. Conscious that she wanted to live this experience not alone but in communion with others who also had embraced the gospel, she stayed close to friends by sharing phone calls, visits, gifts and letters. She refused higher doses of morphine because it dulled her lucidity. But she remained joyful until the moment she died. Chiara Badano inspired everyone who met her by her constant "yes" to Jesus both before and during her illness.

Our natural reaction to events, including suffering, is to analyze them; and there is nothing wrong with this, at least to an extent. It is healthy to try to name what's going on in our lives. We look for reasons, ask ourselves if we could have prevented something from happening. We may even look for meaning via counseling and therapy.

The gospel opens up another avenue—trying to face up to and understand our suffering in the light of the example of Jesus on the cross, in the moment of his most intense suffering.

As one of the stories in this book shows, practicing Christians sometimes feel that their suffering separates them from Jesus, that they are not worthy of his care and mercy. However, he is always present to us. In Matthew 28:20 Jesus assures us, "I am with you always, to the end of the age." Paul confirmed that nothing "… will be able to separate us from the love of God in Christ Jesus our Lord" (Rom 8:39). Recall how Jesus first manifested himself to

Paul when he called himself Saul and was persecuting Christians. On the road to Damascus, Jesus appeared to him and asked, "Saul, Saul, why do you persecute me?" (Acts 9:4). Jesus didn't ask, "Why do you persecute my church?" or "Why do you persecute my followers?" but, "Why do you persecute *me*?" So, even though glorified, Jesus identifies himself with us, his followers, and — as we will see in Step 2 — is present behind any kind of suffering we may experience.

When we transform our questions into moments of entrusting ourselves to Jesus who has made all suffering his own and who is with us, precisely in all our suffering, then we can move forward in many ways, as the following real-life story illustrates.

Real-Life Story
A Barrier-Free World[4]

I have been physically disabled since the age of five when I contracted polio, leaving me paralyzed from the neck down. Through massage and therapy, I regained the use of my arms. I still have memories of feeling abandoned in lonely hospital rooms, of hallways with rows of people in casts or wheelchairs, with crutches and canes — everyone waiting to be seen by the doctor. There were children like me, screaming from the fright and pain of the procedure. Nothing made sense to me and little as I was, I began to wonder about the existence of suffering. Many other children around me were not disabled. Why me?

When I was seven, my parents decided that it was time for me to attend school. My treatment was suspended and I was sent to a parochial school. One of the first things I learned was that the human person was made in the image and likeness of God. I still recall my religion teacher bringing to class a huge picture of Adam and Eve in the Garden of Eden. I stared at it for a long time and noticed that compared to me, Eve had a perfect body. She was beautiful while I was in a wheelchair. Somehow, I could not reconcile this fact within me. As a child, I thought that the only way to be "okay" as a human being was not to be disabled.

It was hard growing up in the mainstream world when you were excluded from physical education class, girl scouting, field trips and camping. I was only encouraged to study. The struggle became even tougher as a teenager since I had no role models to emulate. I wanted to find an adult person with a disability to whom I could relate. To add to my struggle, I was totally excluded from the social scene of my peers. I was very deeply hurt.

Through contact with others who had made the gospel their lifestyle, I discovered a spirituality that would change my life forever. For the first time I felt that God loved me and I was drawn by the discovery of Jesus on the cross, when he experienced abandonment and was so physically unattractive to others. He, like me, was disabled. Through him, I found the answer to my persistent "Why?" The night before he died, he had prayed to his Father: "So that all may be one" (Jn 17:21). He had paid with his life for the unity of men and women. I realized that my suffering could also contribute to uniting people.

This new understanding urged me to change my ways. I resolved to see the positive in everything, even my disability. I learned to recognize the presence of Jesus in each person. As a consequence, I no longer expected my siblings to meet my every need and began to do for myself as much as possible.

I became active in the disability movement (ADAPT[5]) and in 1985 joined the mass demonstration it sponsored in Los Angeles. I rode my wheelchair as we marched, chanting: "Access is a civil right!" Another disabled man rode beside me and every now and then he would stop to quench his thirst. I helped him get some water. I wanted to share my discovery of God's love with other disabled people, but I knew that the only way was to take the initiative in loving.

Once, while speaking at a conference in Michigan, I spoke about my discovery of God's love for me. A group of Jewish people with disabilities later approached me to share how happy they were to hear someone in the disability movement finally speak about spirituality.

Real-Life Story

There are always many occasions to help build bridges, even within the disability community itself. In our group, for example, there was a fierce competition among leaders who had different styles and philosophies. My first attempt to bring about solidarity was to love and propose a new idea of "accessibility," of being like ramps for each other. If we could work for accessible buildings and transportation, I explained, then we should work harder to be "accessible" to each other.

My idea was put to the test when I was verbally attacked by one of the members who sent out a newsletter with inflammatory statements against me. People advised me to fight back with a lawsuit. Instead, I decided to write a letter proposing forgiveness and fraternal access to each other. I sent it out as a mass mailing and received an overwhelming favorable response. In the end, the person who had offended me called to say that he agreed with everything that I had to say.

There are still barriers in our society that cause much pain to people with disabilities; we can still encounter prejudice, lack of job opportunities and accessible environments. We need to work for real social change in order to bring about "equality for all." But even as an activist in the disability community, I am constantly affirming that there is no better solution than that contained in the gospel, where the dignity and worth of every human being is underlined by a God who loves and respects each one of his children.

Step 2
Recognizing the Presence of Jesus in Suffering

Cooperating with Christ

Christianity preaches the infinite worth of that which is seemingly worthless and the infinite worthlessness of that which is seemingly so valued.

Dietrich Bonhoeffer[6]

There is a vocation to suffer with Christ and thereby to cooperate with him in his work of salvation. When we are united with the Lord, we are members of the mystical body of Christ: Christ lives in his members and continues to suffer in them. And the suffering borne in union with the Lord is his suffering, incorporated in the great work of salvation and fruitful therein.

Edith Stein[7]

Recognizing the Presence of Jesus in Suffering

*M*OTHER TERESA OF CALCUTTA "saw" the face of the suffering Christ in the faces of the poorest of the poor. Like her, saints throughout the centuries have seen Jesus in the poor and the ill, and have chosen to serve them. Many religious orders continue this work today.

Chiara Lubich, founder of the Focolare Movement, whose writings and teaching supply the foundation for this book, explains that Jesus knew all of our sufferings so intimately and identified with them so strongly that he *became* Suffering. She says that this happened through his "abandonment" and because of his great love for us. Jesus, fully human and fully divine, took upon himself each and every type of suffering that a human being can experience, each and every kind of cross we may have to bear. He has made all suffering his own.

Are we unappreciated, ignored or overlooked? Have we been hurt, betrayed or abandoned by a loved one? So was Jesus on the cross. Are some children in our country hungry, abused or homeless? In a foreign country ravaged by natural disaster or war, are people—our neighbors—terrorized, injured or dying? So was the crucified Jesus. Are we sometimes powerless to change situations? Do we sometimes fail to help even the ones we hold dearest? Jesus, too, was unable to come down from the cross. He also "failed."

Step 2

When we or our neighbors suffer in any way, we are actually experiencing Jesus behind the mask of that pain, wound, separation, or failure. We can say to him, "You suffered for me? You became this suffering out of love for me? Then I love you back."

We are called to respond to the suffering, which is really Jesus, with love. Our acceptance, our "yes" to Jesus hidden beneath every suffering, especially suffering endured for the sake of others, becomes an act of pure love.

Does this mean that we look for opportunities to suffer? No. Life will naturally present us with those opportunities. Does it mean that we avoid seeking relief for physical or emotional pain, or that we try to prolong it? No. But, when we hurt, our first thought can be accepting it and offering it to the One who suffered for us. Our next act will deal with that hurt in a prudent and healthy way, through any necessary medical or psychological means. One special note: if suffering ever makes us think of harming ourselves or others, then we must call someone for help right away, and keep calling until we get that help. Reaching out is not a sign of weakness, but strength.

There will be times, though, when we *choose* a personal hardship because we love someone, or in order to love our neighbor. For example, a parent may take a second job to better support his or her family. It is only love, the love that comes from God, which can give us the strength to do so. We imitate Jesus by living his words, "No one has greater love than this, to lay down one's life for one's friends" (Jn 15:13). We may not have to lay it down literally, but we may need to lay down our own desires, ideas or egos.

Through Jesus' suffering and death, our sins have been forgiven and our unity with God restored; through his resurrection, we have been given eternal life. Raniero Cantalamessa, OFM Cap., explains the mystery this way: "What do you do to reassure someone that a particular drink contains no poison? You drink it yourself first, in front of him. This is what God has done for humanity: he has drunk the bitter cup of the passion.... At the bottom of the chalice, there must be a pearl. We know the name of that pearl: resurrection!"[8]

Real-Life Story
Jobless in Texas[9]

In September 2008, like so many Americans, I was laid off from my job with no severance package. For the two years leading up to my layoff we had been struggling financially, because my family and I were on one income, which was then barely meeting our needs. All of a sudden we had no income at all.

Step 2

The day my job came to an end I resolved to continue to love God, believing that a solution would soon come about. Many in my spiritual community knew of my suffering and were experiencing it with me in the way that friends try to share your burdens — they prayed for me, and they made the effort to suffer "with" me.

I began job searching, ready to face whatever obstacles might arise, but after many months and running out of money, I began to weaken. One day when I was praying, I wrote down words to describe how I felt: "Scared, sad, confused, desperate, unfulfilled, anxious," and so on. I thought about these emotions and wondered how I could escape the numbness I felt from the power they had over me.

I knew that God is love, and that I needed to continue loving, trying to be available for the needs of those around me. I understood, too, that continuing to love and serve would free me from the numbness I was experiencing.

I began to focus not so much on the painful emotion but on perfecting love in each moment. When I made a phone call, I would say to myself, "Be love." When I washed dishes, "Be love." When I didn't think other family members were doing their part, I thought, "Keep loving." When people were not helpful in my job search, I would try to be helpful to them. Tangible solutions were long in coming, but embracing obstacles in this way made the next moment easier.

When I finally found a job and looked back at each step, I could see that my choice to carry the cross *with* Jesus allowed me to see each new aspect of the difficult situation as an opportunity to love rather than as a new burden to bear. Seeing it this way helped me to "invite" others to share it. I didn't feel like I was inviting them into my misery. Rather, that I invited them into an opportunity to love. It's a radical way of looking at the world! But, it made me see that while "suffering'" is just an idea or an emotion, there is always a "being" behind it or in it who can be loved.

Real-Life Story
Illness, Fear and Love[10]

A few months ago, a relative of mine received the news that her cancer had returned, more aggressive than ever. We have always been very close, growing up together and growing old together.

She was deeply afraid. She felt unworthy of God's mercy and did not think God could ever forgive her for all the mistakes she had made in her life. She would say, "It's hard to live and it's so hard to die." No amount of reasoning could free her from this fear.

Realizing how much she was suffering, I wanted to accompany her on her way. The gospel sentence, "My God, my God, why have you forsaken me?" (Mt 27:46) came to my help. Jesus himself had seemed to doubt the love of the Father in that moment. He, too, had suffered physical and spiritual pain. In this relative of mine, I needed to discover the presence of Jesus and love that presence in her. This would be the only way I could help prepare her for her departure from this earth.

It wasn't always easy. Sometimes she would refuse my help even in little things, like getting her water or fixing her bed covers. One day she even gave me a list of what not to do or say when accompanying her to the hospital. I felt like a child who was to be seen and not heard. I felt hurt by her words. In that moment, I remembered that Jesus on the cross had experienced hurt and felt rejected, too. Yet, he still gave everything to the Father, believing in his love. I, too, needed to do the same and to keep loving in the next moment, as Jesus did with us.

In the long run, I realized that her reactions were a result of the illness and she later apologized for her irritability, assuring me her gratitude for all I was doing for her. Our bond grew, and is now deeper than ever.

As a result of experiencing this suffering together, there is now peace, and gradually she has come to accept God's mercy in her life. In the struggles of every day, she is even helping those around her. Others have noticed a change in her. "I feel like God has forgiven me," she shared recently.

Step 3
Living the Present Moment

**Accepting Suffering
in the Present**

The truth that many people never understand, until it is too late, is that the more you try to avoid suffering the more you suffer because smaller and more insignificant things begin to torture you in proportion to your fear of being hurt.

Thomas Merton [11]

I do not want to foresee the future. I am concerned with taking care of the present. God has given me no control over the moment following.

Mahatma Gandhi [12]

Living the Present Moment

CERTAIN SUFFERINGS MAY BE brief, and others more lasting. No one has courage enough to face weeks, months or years of pain all at once. That's why there is great wisdom in focusing on the present, one moment at a time.

Augustine of Hippo said, "Trust the past to God's mercy, the present to God's love, and the future to God's providence."[13] The past is gone. The future is yet to be. Nothing can be done about either one, because they are not here, they are not now. The only time we have in which to act, and in which we can *love* God and our neighbor as we are called to do, is the present moment. It is much wiser and more effective to act and to love *now* than to lose time agonizing over what happened yesterday or dreading what may happen tomorrow. After all, no one really knows how long he or she will live. So, every moment is precious, even if it is painful. Trying to avoid the pain or push it away can lead at best to escapism and at worst to addictions, depression and suicide.

When we live in the present moment, we are also living with God in eternity, the eternal "Now." God, and his love and mercy, are here, completely available to us, right now. So we can do his will and fulfill our specific vocation, now. Henri J. M. Nouwen offers this reflection in *Can You Drink the Cup?*

Step 3

> When we are committed to do God's will and not our own we soon discover that much of what we do doesn't need to be done by us. What we are called to do is actions that bring us true joy and peace.... Actions that lead to overwork, exhaustion and burnout can't praise and glorify God. What God calls us to do we *can* do and do *well.* When we listen in silence to God's voice and speak with our friends in trust we will know what we are called to do and we will do it with a grateful heart.[14]

Suffering is a mystery. There is no simple answer to the problem of suffering in our lives. And yet, in faith we can say that God permits our suffering somehow for our benefit, because a true father permits only what is good for his children. In Matthew 7:11, Jesus reminds us, "If you then, who are evil, know how to give good gifts to your children, how much more will your Father in heaven give good things to those who ask him!"

Because Jesus' suffering served a higher purpose, so can ours. Unlike Jesus, we may never know exactly God's purpose or plan for our suffering while we are still on earth. But in his *Where Is God When It Hurts?* Phillip Yancey proposes a general purpose for human suffering: the forming of our souls.

In some ways it would be easier for God to step in, to have faith for us, to help us in extraordinary ways. But he has chosen instead to stand before us, arms extended, while he asks us to walk, to participate in our own soul-making. That process always involves struggle, and often involves suffering.

Later in the same work, Yancey states:

We are not put on earth merely to satisfy our desires.... We are here to be changed, to be made more like God in order to prepare us for a lifetime with him.[15]

Imagine: we can actively participate and cooperate with God in our transformation and redemption! How? By living the present moment.

Real-Life Story
I Want What You Want[16]

As a Christian I believe in the value of suffering and that it brings me into a deeper and deeper union with God and everyone around me. At the same time, by nature, I am not the most positive person and I'm inclined to be fearful and impatient when it comes to uncertainties in my life. I prefer solutions! So, when a person like me encounters illness, it is not an easy task.

Recently I was scheduled for surgery for the removal of a polyp on my vocal cord but I first had to get a medical clearance from my cardiologist. After some tests, he cancelled my surgery and scheduled me for an angioplasty before any other procedure could take place. This was the start of a chain of events.

A friend had suggested that I see another doctor for a second surgical opinion. At the first visit with this doctor we sensed her concern. Although we were feeling fearful and anxious about my health, my wife and I agreed to live in the present moment fully and to make an even greater effort to love whomever God put next to us. A few weeks later we received the results of the tests that had been taken and the doctor seemed even more concerned. She wanted to send all the information to a larynx specialist in Boston. Within a short time, he called us saying he had rearranged his surgical schedule and wanted to see me within a few days. The urgency in his voice made us realize things were more serious than we had anticipated. We had never met him but we believed the hand of God was really guiding us.

During the days after that call I was very nervous. In my fear, the Mass seemed to become more meaningful than ever. In his homily one day the priest spoke about trust and in those days I read in the Scriptures, "You of little faith, why did you doubt?" (Mt 14:31). This was a moment of conversion for me. After Mass, Father gave me the anointing of the sick and said a prayer. I felt embraced by God and overwhelmed by his love for me.

We left for Boston and throughout this experience I kept putting my fears aside in order to love my wife and everyone around me. The day before the surgery the doctor told me he was certain I had cancer of the vocal cord, which would have to be removed. This was a big blow! I lost my father, mother and two sisters to cancer so I was very aware of the effects of this disease. It was a moment of deep, deep difficulty, and I was never so scared. I believed God was inviting me to come up on the cross with him. It was a moment of complete surrender to his will and my prayer was, "I want what you want."

After the surgery the doctor told me, "You got here just in time; the cancer was contained in your vocal cord." He removed the cord and said I would not need further treatments. He also did the first procedure for reconstructing the area and I will have another procedure to give more volume to my voice.

In facing my mortality, I have realized that I am powerless over my life. This has always been the reality, but it hadn't hit home until then. I know that other moments of trial will come but I also know that I am not alone. The love of the community living every moment with me brings about the presence of Jesus and, with him, "everything is possible."

I don't put my hope in life itself but, rather, in the love of God in all things. I believe that he is with me in every moment and will give me all I need to complete my journey.

Step 4
Embracing Jesus Crucified and Forsaken

The Depth of the Mystery

In order to bring man back to the Father's face, Jesus not only had to take on the face of man, but he had to burden himself with the "face" of sin.... We shall never exhaust the depths of this mystery. All the harshness of the paradox can be heard in Jesus' seemingly desperate cry of pain on the Cross: ... "My God, my God, why have you forsaken me?" (Mk 15:34). Is it possible to imagine a greater agony, a more impenetrable darkness? ...

Jesus' cry on the Cross, dear Brothers and Sisters, is not the cry of anguish of a man without hope, but the prayer of the Son who offers his life to the Father in love, for the salvation of all. At the very moment when he identifies with our sin, "abandoned" by the Father, he "abandons" himself into the hands of the Father. His eyes remain fixed on the Father.

John Paul II[17]

*S*UFFERING CAN SEEM A complete waste. And yet, Christian faith tells us that we can use suffering as a springboard, a leap toward loving God and also our neighbor in whatever God asks of us now. In 2 Corinthians, Paul asked the Lord to remove an affliction. "[B]ut he said to me, 'My grace is sufficient for you, for power is made perfect in weakness.' So I will boast ... of my weaknesses, so that the power of Christ may dwell in me.... [F]or whenever I am weak, then I am strong" (2 Cor 12:9-10).

If Jesus is with us in suffering, then we can embrace him. No matter how weak or helpless our own pain or that of others makes us feel, we can choose to see him — crucified and forsaken — in "the least" of our brothers and sisters. And since he is Love, we discover that our suffering can be transformed into love. He has made our suffering his own, and because of the strength we receive from embracing Jesus in every suffering, we can also go beyond suffering to love.

After we have said our own yes to Jesus, especially in suffering, we can reach out to others. Often, our own pain gives us compassion for others in pain. We can listen, if they need to talk; we can give advice, if they ask for it; we can pray with them and for them; we can help them if they are in need of food, money, clothing or household items. We could even offer hospitality, especially if they need company, and pleasant conversation. In other words, we can choose to love them.

Of course, there will also be times when it seems that we can do little or nothing for a suffering loved one or neighbor. A loved one may tell us about medical tests indicating cancer but he or she has to wait days for confirmation. Or we may hear that someone we love has had an accident overseas, and we cannot go and be with that person immediately. These situations can make us feel helpless, but there is indeed something we can do.

When we cannot alleviate suffering, our own or someone else's, then we must do what we can with all our love, and trust that our loving, merciful God, who can do more than we can ever do ourselves, will take care of everything else. Whatever we need to do now — praying, cleaning, studying, caring for family members, answering an email or phone call — we concentrate on doing it the best we can, and with love as our motivation. Chiara Lubich has written about this method of living suffering:

> This way the task is being done by two in perfect communion. It demands from us great faith in God's love for his children. And in turn it gives God a chance to trust that we do our part. This mutual trust works miracles. We will realize that Another has accomplished what we could

> not do, and that he has done it far better than we could have.
>
> Then our trust will be rewarded. Our limited life acquires a new dimension: we feel near the infinite for which we yearn. Our faith invigorates and gives our love new strength. We will know loneliness no longer. Since we have experienced it, we will be more deeply aware of being children of a God, who is a father and can do everything.[18]

Again, Jesus provides a perfect example. While he suffered, Jesus continued to love. He forgave the men who nailed him to the cross. Next, to the "good thief" he promised Paradise. Then he thought of Mary, and also his beloved disciple. "When Jesus saw his mother and the disciple whom he loved standing beside her, he said to his mother, 'Woman, here is your son.' Then he said to the disciple, 'Here is your mother.' And from that hour, the disciple took her into his own home" (Jn 19:26-27). People need each other. In fact, psychologists say that having someone to love is essential to a person's happiness. It seems that, because his earthly life was over and they would remain, Jesus gave Mary and his disciple to each other as mother and child, the closest family bond, the one with the strongest love.

By living the present moment well, we will be alert to our own opportunities to go beyond suffering and love the people in front of us.

Real-Life Story
Competing Deadlines[19]

I was working late one night under three deadlines, all of which merged onto the same evening, when a friend called to ask for help on a brochure covering her new dance school. The deadline for that brochure had been scheduled for two days later, but she had just opened her email to find its deadline moved forward.

I wasn't very patient. We went in circles, I trying to fast forward her thoughts, just to get the brochure finished so that I could return to my other work. She, faithful to her own inspiration for her project, persevered patiently, lovingly, explaining that my first suggestion and my next suggestion were not exactly right.

Finally, I stopped. I knew I was not loving.

It was a bad moment: no energy, no focus, no love.

I went inside my soul, showed Jesus my failure, remembered that he had felt failure, and I renewed my love for him.

I apologized. We started over. The ideas flowed. Within a very short time, my friend and I had resolved the crux of the description of her school.

At that moment, we discovered that neither of us had typed out our ideas, thinking the other had been recording them! I took a deep breath. My brain was fried, but a gospel sentence we had talked about recently came to my mind, which said, "… forgive, put ourselves at the service of the others …" Yes, love of neighbor was all that mattered.

I asked the Holy Spirit to give back those very words which together we had drawn up. They came back! The brochure was finished!

Real-Life Story
Unconditional Love for My Daughter[20]

My daughter was a bright student and a very loving child in good health until, coming home one day, she started being unable to sleep and becoming unreasonable and demanding. At school, she began to swear at teachers and the principal, which was very much unlike her. It got so bad that we had to decide to begin home-schooling her.

My husband, who is a physician, and I, a nurse, were unable to pinpoint the problem at first. When our daughter was sixteen we finally consulted a psychiatrist, who diagnosed her as having manic depression, a hereditary illness. A series of many long days and nights began.

In the manic phase of the illness, my scholarly, timid and quiet child became daring, combative and argumentative. In the depressive phase she wanted to end her life. Although medication would prevent her mood swings, she disliked feeling controlled and frequently refused to take the prescriptions. Encouraging and even bribing her to take her pills became a daily battle.

One night she became so combative that we had to make the difficult decision to hospitalize her. With my daughter's troubles now more visible, I had to deal not only with her illness but also with comments from friends and relatives, which were like a sword piercing my heart. People speculated that our daughter was spoiled or on drugs and questioned our decisions.

During this ordeal I was sustained by Christian friends who gave me nonstop, unconditional support. Their loving care gave me the strength to see the presence of Jesus on the cross in my daughter's suffering, to look at her with new eyes every day, and even to accept patiently the critical remarks, realizing that people just had no idea what we were going through.

With intensive therapy and medication, the depression was controlled and my daughter was eventually discharged, seemingly our normal sweet child again. Much to our joy, she was able to finish high school with her classmates.

Aware of the stigma of her illness, she wanted to move far from our home town for college, and we could not convince her to stay. She applied and got admitted to an out-of-state university, and we brought her there, making sure she had all she needed, including a psychiatrist to follow up on her illness.

When she was well she was as sweet as ever, thanking us for taking care of her during her illness. But unfortunately, her improved condition did not last. Within one month, she was so sick again that we had to bring her back home to be hospitalized for two months more.

Following the treatment, she improved again and started to attend the local community college. All seemed well as she graduated with distinction, enabling her to be admitted to university. She obtained a Health Science Degree, specializing in Mental Health and, upon her graduation, worked in a mental health clinic as an administrator. Realizing that she had to turn mentally ill patients away due to deficiencies in existing health care laws, she set out to study law to help people less fortunate than she was.

But the depression was like a time bomb. Before completing her law degree, she was hospitalized once more. Medication, therapy and hospitalization could control her illness, but never cure her. She was engaged to be married and was working in a non-profit law firm for the mentally ill, when three weeks before her wedding our worst fears came true: she committed suicide. Her fiancé called us with the unbelievably shocking news.

Dealing with her loss was the most challenging thing I have ever lived, and it took all my faith in God's love to get through this tragedy. To this day I miss her very much and for the first two years I cried a lot whenever I thought of her. But I made an effort not to focus on what I could have or should have done differently, but to concentrate on the positive fact that now my daughter no longer had to battle with her illness. I repeatedly told myself that God welcomed her home.

Staying connected with my Christian friends and continuing to participate in their community events was vital. I realized that I couldn't be blocked by feeling sorry for myself, much less resort to blaming others like her fiancé or the psychiatrist who had cared for her; I had to reach out to others in turn. As a result, no relationships were broken and her then-fiancé occasionally still calls us.

By continuing to live the gospel command of love and identifying with Jesus on the cross, who gave everything for us, I want to honor my daughter's life, which she dedicated for years to help people in even greater need than she was herself.

Step 5
Going beyond Suffering toward Unity with Our Neighbor

The Way to Love Our Neighbor

Jesus said, "This is my commandment, love one another." But he did not leave this love without a model, for he added, "as I have loved you" (Jn 15:12). And he did not leave this without any explanation when he added further, "There is no greater love than this, to lay down one's life for one's friends" (Jn 15:13).

Yes, Jesus crucified and forsaken is the way to love our neighbor. His death on the cross, forsaken, is the highest, divine, heroic lesson from Jesus about the nature of love ... he is the model of the person who loves; he is the path and key to unity with our neighbors....

Looking at him we understand how everything is to be given or put aside for love of our neighbors. The things of this earth ... and in a certain way — should it be necessary — also the things of heaven.... Ready to leave God, for example, in prayer, to "make ourselves one" with someone in need.

Chiara Lubich[21]

JESUS CAME INTO THE world to reconcile us to God. We also need to be reconciled to each other. In 1 John 4:20-21, we are told, "... those who do not love a brother or sister, whom they have seen, cannot love God whom they have not seen. The commandment we have from him is this: Those who love God must love their brothers and sisters also."

At the Last Supper, Jesus prayed to the Father for all of us: "I ask not only on behalf of these, but also on behalf of those who will believe in me through their word, that they may all be one. As you Father, are in me and I am in you, may they also be in us, so that the world may believe that you have sent me ... so that they may ... become completely one, so that the world may know that you have sent me and have loved them even as you have loved me" (Jn 17:20-23). Jesus wants our complete unity. Through that unity, everyone can come to know that God loves him or her just as the Father loves his Son. Our ultimate goal as Christians is unity with our neighbor, regardless of age, race, creed, nationality or culture, unity in all things except sin.

Let's pause for a moment to reflect on our situations. We are so used to "having" that we sometimes become complacent about it. If our electricity is suddenly cut off we might wonder what to do without a TV or computer. Yet, in another country, our neighbors have no choice but to live without any electricity. If our faucets stop running we might immediately call the water company, demanding to know why we have been so inconvenienced. Meanwhile, half a world away, people walk for miles to fill plastic jugs with water for their families. If we get sick we might call a medical office, expecting to see a doctor today. In other places, our gravely ill brothers and sisters have no one to call, no doctor, no medicine.

Although news from around the globe is available almost instantly, we can lose perspective and be passive about the needs of others. "Well, there's little or nothing I can do to help them. I can't make a difference." This isn't always a conscious choice or decision, of course. It may be due to information overload, to hearing about disasters and tragedies happening nearly everywhere and at every hour. Technology "connects" us and yet can leave us insulated from events or even isolated from other people. So, we may tune things out or quickly forget them. But what if the things or people that matter most to *us* are suddenly scarce or gone?

Then we feel their lack and understand — perhaps too late — just what we had. It often takes losing a right, a blessing or a loved one to make us truly appreciate them. Any loss, hardship, illness or pain can act as a prompt, a catalyst to reach out and love our neighbors, trying to understand them, as Jesus did and wants us to imitate. There may indeed be times when we can do very little or nothing, but as it has been pointed out: "No one can do everything, but everyone can do something."

In the first four steps, we have moved beyond the "Why" to recognize Jesus in suffering, focusing on living the present moment well, and trying to embrace Jesus, crucified and forsaken. Now we can go beyond suffering and try to understand our neighbor's situation, walk "in his or her shoes," so to speak.

Paul explains in Philippians 2:6-8 that Jesus who, though he was in the form of God, did not regard equality with God something to be exploited, but emptied himself, taking the form of a slave, being born in human likeness. And being found in human form, he humbled himself and became obedient to the point of death — even death on a cross.

Then in 1 Corinthians 9:22, Paul gives his own example of empathizing with his neighbors: "To the weak I became weak, so that I might win the weak. I became all things to all people, so that I might by any means save some."

Jesus, too, identified with us in our joys and sorrows, which means that to imitate Jesus, we need to unite ourselves to others, anyone who might be in front of us, sharing — entering into — their joy or sorrow.

Civil War chaplain, pastor and author E. M. Bounds said, "All God's plans have the mark of the cross on them, and all His plans have death to self in them."[22] Death to self can be extremely challenging. But, if we keep Jesus crucified and forsaken as our focus, we can receive the grace to love even in moments of great suffering. We can imagine ourselves in someone else's place and ask ourselves, "How would I want to be loved in this moment?" Then, we can give.

Our gift to another might be as simple as a friendly greeting or a smile. And yet, even a small thing can brighten someone's outlook, spark hope, and help that person feel less frightened or alone. Knowing that another human being understands and stands beside me can bring comfort even in the bleakest moments.

When we can transform our suffering into love, we become a sign and instrument of Jesus' love. By uniting ourselves in love to one neighbor at a time, we reach the fullness of our journey: unity with God in Jesus, and with our neighbors.

Love frequently generates more love, although we must not anticipate "results." When we love for Love's own sake, expecting nothing in return, then we truly love. When we truly love someone, that person may also love us in return. This mutual love brings comfort, consolation, and often unity. It transforms our suffering into joy.

Real-Life Story
An Enduring Love[23]

Rose: I woke up one morning with a numbness from my waist down. I was immediately hospitalized and had to undergo many painful tests. I remember saying to God that I wanted to be ready for anything that he was going to ask of me. At the same time, I felt a certain fear in not knowing what was happening to my body. Initially, I was diagnosed as having an unknown virus, but after subsequent attacks and further hospitalizations, I was gently told by my doctors that I had Multiple Sclerosis (MS). At first those words left me stunned. I asked Jesus to give me the courage to say yes to what he was asking of me.

Howard: When I first heard the word MS, I thought of all the people I had known with it and the crippling effects it had on them. I felt sick at the thought that this could happen to Rose, but I knew I could not let her feel my fear. While together in the hospital, we talked about these changes in our life. We held firmly to the conviction that God loves us as a Father, and in some way this was a gift for our family.

Rose: Even with Howard's support and love and my whole-hearted yes to God, there were many adjustments to be made. I found myself experiencing multiple side effects from the medication. I struggled with sadness, anxiety, doubts, even bouts of depression, which I had never experienced before. I was beginning to feel alone and forsaken. I did not want to give in to these feelings but at times they were so strong that I felt I could not control them, and this too frightened me. I realized that in my own small measure I was experiencing something of what Jesus must have experienced when he felt abandoned on the cross.

One day in the hospital, as I struggled to conquer one of those moments, I glanced over at the bed next to mine where someone had recently arrived. I had been so wrapped up in my own concerns that I had totally lost sight of who was next to me. I introduced myself and we began to converse. I listened while she described all her problems and I felt a great peace come into my soul and my own suffering slowly disappeared. Looking back, I realize that this was the turning point in my life.

Howard: I could see Rose was greeting people at the hospital with love, not looking for any sympathy. This gave me the courage to do the same. I found myself with many things to do: drive our five sons to their different activities, do the shopping and so on. Her illness was forcing us to change both our lives. But I realized the changes she had to make were so much greater than mine. She had been an outgoing person, involved in the activities of the children and capable of handling a lot of responsibility. Now she had to give up many of these commitments. Her ability to do what God seemed to want from her as expressed by this illness amazed me. She was still the same person and simply organized herself to deal with her illness, following all the directives from her doctor. He had told her she should rest two hours, then she could work two hours. If I came home early for lunch, I'd say, "Let's eat," and she would answer, "Ten minutes more." Then she would get up and because she was so organized, would accomplish a great deal, like making herself available to our five boys, cooking meals, doing the laundry and being a comfort with her listening ear to me and all those who called or visited our home. When I came home from work exhausted or preoccupied, I would open the door to find her there welcoming me with her beautiful smile, as if she had no other concern but to be there totally for me. This melted my heart and made me forget all my burdens.

Rose: Notwithstanding the many difficult moments and obstacles to overcome, there were also many joys in our lives. In the midst of taking care of the family to the best of my ability, I sensed God's love taking care of me. After years of going to the hospital after every attack and being treated intravenously, I was able to get connected with a specialist who successfully treated me with an oral medication. I continued to get attacks, but less and less severe and I have been in remission for the past several years.

Howard: Rose would often tell me, "I have to listen to what my body is telling me," and she would stop in the middle of something and lie down. At another time she would say, "Yes, I can make that appointment."

Despite Rose's low physical endurance, our boys grew up hardly noticing that Rose had MS. She was always there for them, never letting them feel it. As a result they matured in a very balanced and wholesome way. I see that this experience has given them the ability to be more sensitive and compassionate to others. What initially seemed like a tragedy has become an enrichment for the whole family, a gift from God, I would say, that changed our whole lives. The difficulties and sufferings were turned into love.

Notes

1. William H. Gentz, ed., Dictionary of Bible and Religion (Nashville, TN.: Abingdon Press, 1986), p. 335.
2. Dennis Billy, *Tending the Mustard Seed: Living the Faith in Today's World* (Hyde Park, NY: New City Press, 2013), pp. 67-68. William H. Gentz, ed., *Dictionary of Bible and Religion* (Nashville, TN.: Abingdon Press, 1986), p. 335.
3. C.S. Lewis, *The Problem of Pain* (San Francisco: Harper 2001), pp. 86–87.
4. As shared by Lillibeth Crucis Navarro.
5. American Disabled for Accessible Public Transport, now known as American Disabled for Attendant Programs Today.
6. Dietrich Bonhoeffer, *The Cost of Discipleship* (New York, NY: Simon and Schuster, 1959), p. 41.
7. Edith Stein, *Self Portrait in Letters*, trans. Josephine Koeppel, (Washington D.C.: ICS, 1993), p. 128.
8. October 2012, *The Word Among Us* (Frederick, MD: Word Among Us, 2012), p. 28.

Notes

9. As shared by Martha C. (who asked to remain anonymous).
10. As shared by L.M. (who asked to remain anonymous).
11. Thomas Merton, *Seven Story Mountain* (New York, NY: Houghton Mifflin Harcourt, 1998), p. 91.
12. Mohandas Ghandi, *Young India Newsletter*, Vol. 427, Dec. 24, 1926.
13. Attributed to St. Augustine, *Westminster Collection of Christian Quotations* (Louisville KY: Westminster John Knox, 2001), p. 383.
14. Henri J. M. Nouwen, *Can You Drink the Cup?* (Notre Dame, IN: Ave Maria Press, 1996), pp. 110–11.
15. Phillip Yancey, *Where Is God When It Hurts?* (Grand Rapids, MI: Zondervan, 1990), pp. 87–88.
16. As shared by Leon De Maille.
17. John Paul II, *Novo Millennio Ineunte* (Rome, Italy: Libreria Editrice Vaticana, 2001) pp. 25–26.
18. Chiara Lubich, *Here and Now* (Hyde Park, NY: New City Press, 2005), p. 37.
19. As shared by M. A. (who asked to remain anonymous).
20. As shared by S. S. (who asked to remain anonymous).
21. Chiara Lubich, *Jesus: The Heart of His Message: Unity and Jesus Forsaken* (Hyde Park, NY: New City Press, 1985), pp. 93–94.

22. Edward M. Bounds, *Guide to Spiritual Warfare* (New Kensignton, PA: Whitaker House, 1984), p. 52.
23. As shared by Rose and Howard Belcher.

New City Press
of the Focolare
Hyde Park, New York

New City Press is one of more than 20 publishing houses sponsored by the Focolare, a movement founded by Chiara Lubich to help bring about the realization of Jesus' prayer: "That all may be one" (John 17:21). In view of that goal, New City Press publishes books and resources that enrich the lives of people and help all to strive toward the unity of the entire human family. We are a member of the Association of Catholic Publishers.

Further Reading
All titles are available from New City Press.
www.NewCityPress.com

Other Books in the 5 Step Series:
...to Effective Student Leadership	978-1-56548-509-9	$4.95
...to Living Christian Unity	978-1-56548-501-3	$4.95
...to Positive Political Dialogue	978-1-56548-507-5	$4.95

Titles by Chiara Lubich:
Cry of Jesus Crucified and Forsaken	978-1-56548-159-6	$11.95
Essential Writings	978-1-56548-259-3	$24.95
Jesus: The Heart of His Message	978-1-56548-090-2	$8.95

Scan to join our mailing list for discounts and promotions

Periodicals
Living City Magazine, www.livingcitymagazine.org